W9-AUA-085

Castles

Towers, Dungeons, Moats, and More

by Matt White

Reading Consultant:
Timothy Rasinski, Ph.D.
Professor of Reading Education
Kent State University

Content Consultant:
Brian K. Davison
Archeologist
Former Inspector of
Ancient Monuments
United Kingdom

Red Brick™ Learning

Published by Red Brick™ Learning
7825 Telegraph Road, Bloomington, Minnesota 55438
http://www.redbricklearning.com

Copyright © 2003 Red Brick™ Learning. All rights reserved.

Library of Congress Cataloging-in-Publication Data
White, Matt, 1955–
    Castles: towers, dungeons, moats, and more/by Matt White; reading
consultant, Timothy Rasinski.
    p. cm.—(High five reading)
    Summary: Provides an overview of the history of castles--their origins,
construction, uses, defense, and the daily life of their inhabitants—with an
emphasis on famous castles of the Middle Ages.
    Includes bibliographical references (p. 46) and index.
    ISBN 0-7368-9527-2 (pbk.)—ISBN 0-7368-9549-3 (hard)
    1. Castles—Juvenile literature. 2. Civilization, Medieval—Juvenile
literature. [1. Castles. 2. Civilization, Medieval.] I. Title. II. Series.
GT3550 .W48 2002
940.1—dc21
                                        2002002066

Created by Kent Publishing Services, Inc.
Executive Editor: Robbie Butler
Designed by Signature Design Group, Inc.

This publisher has made every effort to trace ownership of all copyrighted
material and to secure necessary permissions. In the event of any questions
arising as to the use of any material, the publisher, while expressing regret for
any inadvertent error, will be happy to make necessary corrections.

Photo Credits:
Page 4, Historical PictureArchive/Corbis; page 7, Pawel Libera/Corbis; page
11, Johnathan Blair/Corbis; pages 8, 43, Patrick Ward/Corbis; page 9,
Angelo Hornak/Corbis; page 12, Chinch Gryniewicz, Ecoscene/Corbis;
page 15, Charles Shaw/Craven Design; page 19, Yiorgos Nikiteas, Eye
Ubiquitous/Corbis; pages 20, 25, 29, 30 (top), 36, 37, Hulton/Archive by
Getty Images; page 26, Achivo Iconografico, S.A./Corbis; pages 30 (bottom),
34, The Granger Collection; page 33, Bettmann/Corbis; page 39, Corbis; page
40, Michael Nicholson/Corbis; page 41, Adam Woolfitt/Corbis; page 42,
John & Dallas Heaton/Corbis

No part of this book may be reproduced without written permission from the
publisher. The publisher takes no responsibility for the use of any of the mate-
rials or methods described in this book, nor for the products thereof.

Printed in the United States of America.

1 2 3 4 5 6 08 07 06 05 04 03

Table of Contents

William the Conqueror

CHAPTER 1

The Tower of London

Have you heard of the Tower of London? This famous castle was built nearly 1,000 years ago. Many kings and queens stayed there. Many prisoners ate their last meal there, too. Who built it? Why was it built? Read on to find out.

An Enemy Attack

In the 11th century, the Duke of Normandy and his army **invaded** England. They beat the English at the Battle of Hastings in 1066. Soon, they marched on to London.

In London, the duke made himself king of England. The duke's name was William. But the English called him *William the* **Conqueror**.

---

invade: to send an army into a country to take it over
conqueror: a person who defeats an enemy by force

From Corral to Castle

William's army included **knights**. These knights rode fine war horses. To protect these horses, the **Normans** built guarded **corrals**. Some of the corrals grew into forts.

Twelve years after his invasion, William decided he needed a large fort. He had one built in a corner of London, on the River Thames. This fort was the beginning of the Tower of London.

Castles like the Tower of London were built to protect those inside. They kept people and animals safe from attack. Troops inside the castle also could control the land outside the castle walls. William built many castles in England for these reasons. But the Tower of London is his most famous castle.

knight: a man given rank by a king or other noble lord. In return, the knight swore to fight for this king or lord.
Norman: someone from Normandy, which today is part of northern France
corral: a fenced area that holds horses

The White Tower is the most famous part of the Tower of London.

Forts before Castles

The Normans led the way in castle building. But they did not build the earliest castles. Hundreds of years earlier, the Romans built forts all over Europe, including in England.

These forts housed troops and supplies. Like William, the Romans built forts to control the people in lands they had conquered. In fact, William built the Tower of London on the site of old Roman walls.

The ruins of an ancient Roman fort built in England

Two stone walls were added to The Tower of London after the White Tower was built.

Adding On

For about 100 years, the Tower of London stayed the same. Then in 1190, builders added two stone walls and a **moat** around it. This gave more **protection** from enemies. Over the next several hundred years, the fort grew to cover 18 acres (7.3 hectares).

---

moat: a deep, wide ditch filled with water
protection: safety from danger

Still Called Home

The Tower of London housed as many as 1,000 **residents** at a time. These included lords, knights, soldiers, servants, cooks, blacksmiths, and prisoners.

Today, about 150 people live in the Tower of London. It's now a museum. Some people live there to guard it. These guards are called the *Yeoman Warders of the Tower.*

The Tower also houses many treasures. These include the Crown Jewels. English rulers collected these treasures over hundreds of years. The Warders guard these treasures.

Some Warders give Tower tours to visitors. The Warders dress in red and black uniforms. They have another name besides Warders—*Beefeaters.* How do you think they got this name?

---

resident: someone who lives in a place

*A Yeoman Warder locks the door to the Tower of London.
This "Ceremony of the Keys" has been held every night for
more than 700 years.*

Castles: the Real Story

Today, nearly 1,000 years later, the Tower
of London remains a castle. People still
live and work there. But the earliest castles
did not look like the Tower of London
at all.

A 13th-century castle

CHAPTER 2

What Is a Castle?

Think of castles. What do you imagine? Most people think of high stone walls, a moat filled with water, and knights on horseback. But castles went through many changes over time.

A Fort and a Home

A castle had to be strong to defend against attacks. But it also had to be a home to those who lived there.

Several types of castles appeared between the 11th and 14th centuries. What did the first castles look like? How did castles change? Why did they change?

Motte and Bailey Castle

The Normans needed a quick way to defend their conquered lands. The motte and bailey castle met this need.

To build these castles, workers first dug a deep ditch. They piled the earth from this ditch into a high mound. This mound was called a *motte* (MOT). Next, the workers cut trees to build a tower on the motte. They also built a wooden wall, called a *palisade,* around the motte.

Next to the motte, workers made a lower **courtyard**, called the *bailey.* For this, they dug a second ditch farther from the motte. They often filled this outer ditch with water. They built a wall along this second ditch. The bailey stretched between the motte and the wall of the second ditch. In the bailey were stables, workshops, a hall, storerooms, and a chapel.

A person had to cross a bridge over the outer ditch to enter the bailey. A gate with guards also protected the bailey entrance.

---

courtyard: an open area surrounded by walls

Motte and bailey castle

Stone Is Stronger than Wood

By the 11th and 12th centuries, people were making castles of stone. First, they built a simple stone tower on the ground or a low mound. Then, they built stone walls around the tower.

Sometimes, there wasn't any stone nearby the building **site**. To move the stone took a lot of time, money, and hard work. Stone was also much harder than wood to cut and shape. These stone castles took 10 to 20 years to build.

But stone is also much stronger than wood. Stone made it harder to attack the castle. Attackers could not burn down a stone castle. Stone made castles and those inside much safer.

---

site: a place where something is being built

An 11th-century stone castle

The Classic Castle

By the 14th century, castles had become very good protection. **Battlements** topped walls and towers. Beneath battlements, "murder holes" allowed soldiers to drop stones or pour boiling water on attackers.

To enter a castle, people had to cross a **drawbridge** over the moat. This bridge could be raised in time of attack. Behind the drawbridge, a portcullis (port-KUH-liss) gave further protection. This wooden grate had spikes at the base. Soldiers used ropes to raise and lower the portcullis.

Castles took centuries to become the **strongholds** of the 14th century. But why did people need castles anyway? Why did kings and lords have to defend themselves?

---

classic: typical or a perfect example
battlement: the notched stonework on top of a castle wall or tower
drawbridge: a bridge that can be raised to keep someone from crossing
stronghold: a place that is well protected from attack

Built in 1386, the Bodiam Castle was protected by a moat.

In this painting, a medieval lord looks after his estate.

CHAPTER 3

Why Build a Castle?

*Today, a person needs a **permit** to build a home. In the **Middle Ages**, a **noble** had to ask his king for permission to build a castle. Why do you think he needed to ask before building?*

Kings Needed Help

During the Middle Ages, Europe was divided into many small nations. These nations often fought with each other. Kings had to defend their lands.

Kings gave land to nobles. Kings also had certain nobles keep troops. These nobles built castles. They promised to be **loyal** to the king. With their castles and troops, they protected the king and helped him control his lands.

---

permit: a written statement giving permission for something
Middle Ages: a time in Europe between A.D. 500 and 1450
noble: a person of high birth or high rank
loyal: firm in support; faithful

The Feudal System

The King
The king gave land to his most important noblemen. William the Conqueror had 120 barons at his service.

Barons
Barons were the most powerful and wealthy noblemen. In time of war, they provided soldiers to the king.

Bishops
Bishops sometimes had as much power as barons. Many of them were very rich from collections from members of the church.

Lords
Lords received land from the barons. Lords rented most of their land to peasants who worked for them.

Peasants
Peasants worked for the lord and mostly farmed the land. They had few rights.

Europe in the Time of Castles

During the Middle Ages, people were organized by the feudal system. In this system, the king had the most power. After the king came church leaders and nobles.

The king split his land among his chosen nobles. In return, these nobles promised to be loyal to the king. Nobles who reported to the king were called *barons.*

Barons gave land to **lesser** lords. In return, the lesser lords supplied troops for the barons. Like barons, these lords were allowed to build castles. But no one below a lesser lord could have a castle.

These gifts of land made a line of power. Lords were loyal to barons. Barons were loyal to the king. Each man took orders from the next man up the power line. And each man had to lead his troops in battle for his "boss." In this way, the king kept the kingdom under control.

---

lesser: less important

Where to Build

Kings and barons built castles where they needed them to protect and control land. Often this was near a town. Kings and barons chose carefully the building site for their castles.

Water was important. There had to be water nearby. Each horse drank about eight gallons (30 liters) a day! Castles also needed food supplies nearby. Farm workers had to deliver crops back to the castle easily. They also needed to race quickly back inside the castle in times of attack.

But castles were rarely attacked. Mostly, people came and went daily from castles for other reasons. Castles were the **government** and business centers of their area. So again, castles had to be easy to get to.

But what was life like inside the castle walls? Who lived and worked there? What jobs did people do? Read the next chapter to find out.

---

government: the people who rule a country, state, or organization

This medieval castle built at the top of a hill
can only be entered through two gates.

— Chapter **4** —

Life Inside a Castle

What was daily life like in a medieval castle? Were there always battles and war? Or was it mostly parties and fun? Sometimes there were battles, it's true. And sometimes there were parties. But mostly, daily life in a castle was not very exciting at all.

A painting of a medieval lord and lady

Waking Up in a Castle

It's early morning. Fresh guards take over from the night **watch** on the walls and towers. Servants light fires in the Great Hall and kitchen.

The lord and lady awake. They put on underclothes. They wash in cold water, then put on long-sleeved **tunics**. Over these go **mantles**. They fasten these cloaks with a **brooch** near the neck.

After worship in the chapel, it is time for breakfast. The lord and lady have this light meal in the bedroom. So do their guests. The servants grab a bite in the kitchen. There is no family meal at breakfast time.

---

watch: guards who keep a lookout
tunic: a loose gown
mantle: a loose cloak without sleeves
brooch: a large pin worn as a decoration near the neck

Medieval Food

It is now late morning. Noise and smells fill the castle kitchen. The cook and his staff begin to prepare food for the day.

In the kitchen, everyone is busy. A kitchen boy turns meat on a **spit**. Beef, **mutton**, pork, and **poultry** are all cooked this way. In huge iron pots, stews and soups cook.

Every meal includes bread. The lord, lady, and any guests eat from metal plates. Others in the castle eat their food from flat pieces of stale bread. These "trenchers" soak up the meats' juices.

Today, the cook has made puddings from milk, eggs, and fruit. On the table, bowls hold piles of fresh fruit from the **orchard**.

The harpist tunes his harp. Music is played at mealtimes. Many medieval castles had their own harpist and **minstrels**.

---

spit: a pointed rod used to cook meat over a fire
mutton: the flesh of a sheep
poultry: fowl such as chickens and geese raised for food
orchard: an area where fruit trees are grown
minstrel: a performer who travels from place to place

Musicians play for a medieval family at dinner.

A knight and squire hunt with a large dog.

Noblemen tilting. This sport helped train men for the battlefields of medieval Europe.

A Noble Day

During the day, the lord meets with his **stewards** and **bailiffs**. Later he will travel to the villages to see that everything is running smoothly. He will also go hunting with his male guests.

Knights and their **squires** practice fencing or tilting. Tilting is combat on horseback. To tilt, two riders charge at each other, their **lances** held low. The object is to knock your **foe** from his horse.

A **chaplain** teaches the children. After lessons, the children play games. Medieval toys include balls, spinning tops, and dolls. Today the boys do archery. Skill with bow and arrows will be useful in times of war.

Today the castle's guests include two women. Normally, the only women in the castle are the lord's wife and daughters, and a woman who washes clothes.

steward: a person hired to run a large estate
bailiff: an officer who has charge of prisoners
squire: a young man who assists a knight
lance: a long spear used by soldiers
foe: an enemy, or in this case, the other player
chaplain: a person who leads religious services

The Castle at Work

The stable boy's day begins before daybreak. He sweeps out the many stables. Then he brings fresh straw for the horses.

The blacksmith lights his fire early. He has many horseshoes to make today. He also makes chains for the dungeon's prisoners.

In the castle, male servants empty **chamber pots**. Then they sweep rooms and lay fresh **rushes** on the floor.

In the yard, a horse-drawn cart brings vegetables from the fields. The cook sends a servant to net fish in the castle pond.

Men-at-arms sharpen arrowheads and sword blades. They check their bowstrings and oil their metal helmets. The castle is at peace, but an attack can happen at any time. It pays to be prepared.

---

chamber pot: a container used as a toilet in the bedroom
rush: a grassy plant
men-at-arms: soldiers

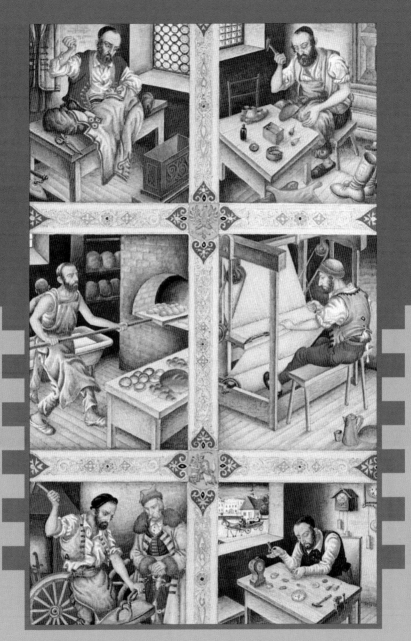

Medieval craftsmen (clockwise from top left): tailor; shoemaker; weaver; clockmaker; blacksmith; baker

— CHAPTER **5** —

Castle Attack

*"There, Baron, beside that wood.
Do you see the enemy?" The knight
points toward the forest.*

*"Aye," says the Baron. "Raise the
alarm. Now, pull up the drawbridge.
Be quick, we have little time."*

*"And look," adds the knight.
"They cut trees. They may be building
attack weapons."*

The storming of a French castle, 15th century

Siege or Direct Attack?

Attackers had two ways to defeat those in a castle. They could attack with weapons and men. Or they could lay siege to the castle.

To lay siege, attackers stopped food and other supplies from going into the castle. Siege armies also used other **tactics**. They might throw dead animals over castle walls. This brought sickness and **disease** into the castle.

Starvation or disease might force the lord of the castle to give up. But a siege might take months. Sometimes the enemy used a direct attack instead.

What weapons might attackers use? How might a foe attack the castle walls and gates? Read on to find out.

---

tactic: a plan to win a battle
disease: an illness or sickness
starvation: suffering or dying because of a lack of food

Weapons of Attack

Enemy builders might make a balista to use in an attack. This weapon looked like a giant crossbow. The balista shot heavy arrows, stones, or burning coals.

Attackers also might make a mangonel (MAN-goh-nell). Twisted ropes were fixed to a long beam. When the ropes were let go, they untwisted quickly. The beam shot up, throwing stones or other objects.

Or they could make a trebuchet (treb-ya-SHET). This weapon had a heavy weight on one end of a long arm. The weight made the arm swing up, throwing a heavy object. Large stones and even dead horses were thrown!

Soldiers prepare to fire a mangonel.

Fighting Back

How did the castle fight back? Archers fired arrows through slits in the walls. From battlements, soldiers threw stones down on the enemy. Through murder holes, they dropped heavy weights. Sometimes they poured boiling water through these holes.

Castles could stand up to many kinds of attacks. Attackers often failed to take the castle. But the gunpowder age brought a new danger. Cannons and guns soon made castles go out of style.

Soldiers load baskets of stones on to a trebuchet behind the walls of a castle.

Gunpowder Changes Things

Castles were made to stand up to swords, lances, and longbows. They were not made for guns and cannons. Armies began to use guns in the late 14th century. In the 15th century, armies had cannons that fired iron balls a long way. By the late 15th century, some cannons could shatter castle walls.

So castles became less and less useful in war. Kings now wanted armies that could move around quickly and use guns. They did not depend on barons' castles anymore. By the 16th century, the age of castles was over. Many castles fell into **ruin**.

Thankfully, some castles survived. You can still walk along a castle wall or look through an arrow slit.

What do you see? **Glimpses** of archers and armored knights? Glimpses of trebuchets throwing huge stones? Glimpses of the age of castles?

---

ruin: the remains of something destroyed
glimpse: a quick look

Tourists visit Windsor Castle.

Epilogue

Castles around the World

Rochester, England

This castle was built around 1112. Its tower is 133 feet (41 meters) tall. It stood up to a siege in 1215, but was badly damaged and later repaired. By 1400, it was out of date and too costly to repair. Today, it has no roof or floor. Still, Rochester is a fine example of a castle from the past.

Rochester

Langeais, France

Langeais was built in Loire, France around 1000. It is the earliest remaining castle with square towers in northern Europe.

Langeais

Alcazar, Spain

King Alfonso VI built Alcazar in Spain in the late 11th century. The castle was rebuilt in the 1350s. Builders made the castle walls stronger by rounding some of the towers.

Alcazar

Eltz

Eltz, Germany

The Counts of Eltz began their huge castle on the River Moselle in Germany in 1157. This castle was added on to between 1200 and 1500.

Glossary

bailiff: an officer who has charge of prisoners

battlement: the notched stonework on top of a castle wall or tower

brooch: a large pin worn as a decoration near the neck

chamber pot: a container used as a toilet in the bedroom

chaplain: a person who leads religious services

classic: typical or a perfect example

conqueror: a person who defeats an enemy by force

corral: a fenced area that holds horses

courtyard: an open area surrounded by walls

disease: an illness or sickness

drawbridge: a bridge that can be raised to keep someone from crossing

foe: an enemy, or in this case, the other player

glimpse: a quick look

government: the people who rule a country, state, or organization

invade: to send an army into a country to take it over

knight: a man given rank by a king or other noble lord. In return, the knight swore to fight for this king or lord.

lance: a long spear used by soldiers

lesser: less important

loyal: firm in support; faithful

mantle: a loose cloak without sleeves

men-at-arms: soldiers

Middle Ages: a time in Europe between A.D. 500 and 1450

minstrel: a performer who travels from place to place

moat: a deep, wide ditch filled with water

mutton: the flesh of a sheep

noble: a person of high birth or high rank

Norman: someone from Normandy, which today is part of
    northern France

orchard: an area where fruit trees are grown

permit: a written statement giving permission for something

poultry: fowl such as chickens and geese raised for food

protection: safety from danger

resident: someone who lives in a place

ruin: the remains of something destroyed

rush: a grassy plant

site: a place where something is being built

spit: a pointed rod used to cook meat over a fire

squire: a young man who assists a knight

starvation: suffering or dying because of a lack of food

steward: a person hired to run a large estate

stronghold: a place that is well protected from attack

tactic: a plan to win a battle

tunic: a loose gown

watch: guards who keep a lookout

Bibliography

Platt, Richard. *Castle*. Stephen Biesty's Cross-Sections. New York: DK Publishing, 1994.

Bergin, Mark. *Castle*. Fast Forward. Danbury, Conn.: Franklin Watts, 1999.

Gravett, Christopher. *Castle*. Eyewitness Books. New York: DK Publishing, 2000.

Gravett, Christopher. *Knight*. Eyewitness Books. New York: DK Publishing, 2000.

Hicks, Peter. *How Castles Were Built*. The Age of Castles. Austin, Texas: Raintree Steck-Vaughn, 1999.

MacDonald, Fiona. *A Medieval Castle*. Inside Story. New York: Peter Bedrick Books, 1990.

Useful Addresses

English Heritage
23 Savile Row,
London W1S 2ET
England UK

The National Trust
36 Queen Anne's Gate,
London SW1H 9AS
England UK

Internet Sites

British Castles
www.castles-of-britain.com/castle6.htm

Castle Battles
www.britannia.com/history/david1.html

English Heritage
www.english-heritage.org.uk

Historic Royal Palaces
www.hrp.org.uk

The National Trust
www.nationaltrust.org.uk

Welsh Castles
www.castlewales.com/home.html

Index